WHAT TO SUBSTITUTE FOR
SEX

WHAT
TO
SUBSTITUTE
FOR

BANTAM BOOKS

NEW YORK · TORONTO · LONDON · SYDNEY · AUCKLAND

SÊX

BARRY SAND

WHAT TO SUBSTITUTE FOR SEX
A Bantam Book / April 1989

Library of Congress Cataloging-in-Publication Data

Sand, Barry.
   What to substitute for sex.

   1. Sex—Humor.   2. Sex (Psychology)—Humor.
I. Title.
PN6162.S255 1989   818'.5402   88-47830
ISBN 0-553-34607-5

Published simultaneously in the United States and Canada

Bantam Books are published by Bantam Books, a division of Bantam
Doubleday Dell Publishing Group, Inc. Its trademark, consisting of
the words "Bantam Books" and the portrayal of a rooster, is Regis-
tered in U.S. Patent and Trademark Office and in other countries.
Marca Registrada. Bantam Books, 666 Fifth Avenue, New York, New
York 10103.

PRINTED IN THE UNITED STATES OF AMERICA

CW   0 9 8 7 6 5 4 3 2 1

FOR GAYLIE

ACKNOWLEDGMENTS

*I would like to thank
Alexandra Penney, Scott McGibbon,
and, of course, Gayle Silverman.*

CONTENTS

ASEXUALITY

DIVERSIONS
WHEN YOU'RE IN THE MOOD
FOR SEX

SUBSTITUTES

Turn–offs

Believe it
OR NOT

Final act

WHAT TO SUBSTITUTE FOR
SEX

ASEXUALITY

Those who choose matrimony do well, and those who choose virginity or voluntary abstinence do better.

POPE JOHN PAUL II, 1982

How does the pope accomplish all the work he wants to do? He doesn't have sex. This is the Lord's way of giving him all the time he needs for dressing, undressing, traveling, spreading the gospel, blessing, praying, and posing for pictures on coffee mugs. Think about your own life. Aren't there lots of things you just don't have time for? If your answer is yes, consider converting to asexuality. It's easier than you think. You don't have to retake your driving test, steroids aren't required, a cash donation is unnecessary, and there's no height requirement. Many influential, talented, and powerful people are asexual. Asexuality is everybody's odds-on favorite for the next trend. So what are you waiting for? Join the Nonsexual Revolution. Read this chapter and take the quiz at the end to find out if you have what it takes to get on the A-list.

ASEXUAL ROLE MODELS

JESUS CHRIST 4 B.C.–A.D. 28

Much is known about his Second Coming—nothing is known about his first.

SAINT THERESA 1515–1582

She ran away from home at the age of seven to seek martyrdom among the Moors. What else can one say? She became a Carmelite nun in 1534, then Mother Superior of the order, and opened seventeen new convents in a unique franchise agreement with God. As for her martyrdom, it never came—and neither did she.

JOAN OF ARC 1412–1431

Joan began hearing the voices of saints at age thirteen. By sixteen, they were giving her recipes, tax tips, and military advice. She led French troops to victory at Orléans, but shortly thereafter was captured and tried. Her spiritual passion set the hearts of her countrymen on fire. To return the favor, they burned her at the stake—the only hot night Joan ever had.

ELIZABETH I 1533–1603

Becoming queen at age twenty-five, Elizabeth I soon built England into a major sea and colonial power. She surrounded herself with a court of witty, handsome young men, all of whom she flirted with and ribaldly teased, but never slept with. Accurately named "The Virgin Queen," from more than one deceiving courtier she took his head, but never gave any.

SIR ISAAC NEWTON 1642–1727

An absentminded, reclusive, devoted scientist, Newton developed the theory of gravity. Working day and night, he sometimes forgot to eat and sleep—but always forgot to make love. Many historians insist he died a virgin. Newton proved his own theory of gravity—he could never get it up.

ORVILLE AND WILBUR WRIGHT 1871–1948; 1867–1912

Inventors of the airplane, the Wright brothers didn't smoke, drink, swear, or lie. They lived at home with their father and sister, never married, and both almost certainly died virgins. The Wrights' first flight lasted twelve seconds—a little longer than an orgasm lasts, but far less dangerous.

GEORGE BERNARD SHAW 1856–1950

Irish-born dramatist, critic, and social reformer, Shaw produced a dozen or so brilliant plays with barbed humor and unconventional wit and won the Nobel Prize for Literature in 1925. Personally, he was shy, prudish, and afraid of intimacy. He didn't lose his virginity until twenty-nine, and the experience so shocked him that he abstained from sex for the next fifteen years. Although his plays thrived, his sex life opened and closed on the same night. Obviously, he couldn't take bad reviews.

J. EDGAR HOOVER 1895–1972

Director of the FBI for forty-eight years, Hoover said, "I was in love once when I was young, but then I became attached to the Bureau." He was also attached to his mother and to Clyde Tolson, an FBI intimate for forty-four years who inherited Hoover's estate. Hoover, however, never made love to anyone. He had opinions on the subject though: "I regret to say that we of the FBI are powerless to act in cases of oral-genital intimacy, unless it has in some way obstructed interstate commerce." When asked by a woman, "Is that a gun in your pocket or are you just glad to see me?" Hoover was one of the few men to respond, "It's a gun, ma'am."

> *Celibacy is never having to say you're boring.*
>
> **GABRIELLE BROWN**
> *The New Celibacy,* **1980**

ASEXUALITY AND YOU

▲ Now that you have some good solid role models, you need to know how you yourself can become asexual. The following guidelines should send you quickly and happily on your way into a new, exciting, and rewarding life completely bereft of sex.

HOW TO BECOME ASEXUAL

1. Immediately cancel any dates you've made.

2. Get your hair cut like John Chancellor's—whether you're a man or a woman.

3. Wear loose, baggy clothes—shapeless enough so that at least once a week someone incorrectly identifies your gender.

4. Just for tax purposes, keep a record of your true gender in your files.

5. Substitute thoughts about the Dewey decimal system or router saws for sexual thoughts.

6. Adopt some cats—a few more than most people consider "eccentric." Neuter them yourself.

7. Stop working out. Why bother? No one will ever see your body again.

8. Keep your refrigerator well stocked. If you feel overwhelmed by sexual desire, eat something. The craving will pass and the extra weight will heighten your asexuality.

9. If a sexual scene appears in a movie, simply cover your ears and eyes and sing softly to yourself "You'll Never Walk Alone." Afterward complain to the theater manager.

THE FINANCIAL ADVANTAGES OF ASEXUALITY

1. You will never again spend money on flowers, wine, dinner out, shows, birth control, or hotel rooms on weekends.

2. You can wear old clothes from either of your parents.

3. You will have no huge psychiatrist's bills resulting from bad relationships.

4. You will never have to put a child through orthodontia or Harvard.

5. You can cut your own hair. Whom are you trying to impress?

6. Your apartment no longer needs to look nice for overnight guests.

7. You'll save a small fortune by not taking self-improvement or extension classes where you hoped to meet someone.

MOVIES THAT WILL HELP YOU BECOME ASEXUAL

1. *Looking For Mr. Goodbar*

2. *Lili*

3. *Hello, Dolly!*

4. *Freaks*

5. *Gandhi*

6. *Song of Norway*

7. *Eraserhead*

8. *The Greatest Story Ever Told*

CURRENT ASEXUALS WHOM YOU CAN WRITE TO FOR INFORMATION, GROOMING TIPS, OR ADVICE

His Holiness Pope John Paul II
Apostolic Palace
00120 Vatican City

Mother Theresa
54A Acharya Jagadish Chandra Bose Road
Calcutta 700016, India
Telephone: 24-7115

Ayatollah Ruhollah Khomeini
Madresseh Faizieh, Qom
61 Kuche Yakhchal Ghazi
Qom, Iran

QUIZ:
DO I HAVE WHAT IT TAKES
TO BE ASEXUAL?

1. **I think sex is**
   a) **healthy**
   b) **dirty**
   c) **what was the question?**

2. **Sex has brought me**
   a) **great pleasure and rewarding relationships**
   b) **disease**
   c) **less pleasure than slipping overdue books into the book drop slot before the library opens**

3. **My last sexual experience was**
   a) **last night**
   b) **last week**
   c) **during the Carter administration**

4. **I would describe myself as**
   a) **a lump of dough**
   b) **a small piece of cheese**
   c) **a happy, well-adjusted adult**

5. **My best friends are**
    a) **men**
    b) **women**
    c) **men and women**
    d) **tiny people in my head whose names only I know**

6. **In bed, I would rate myself as**
    a) **a fox**
    b) **a stallion**
    c) **a slug**

7. **If I could save the world by giving up sex, I would.**
    a) **true**
    b) **false**

8. **If, by giving up sex, I could keep Jerry Lewis from ever appearing on television again, I would.**
    a) **true**
    b) **false**

9. **When I look at myself in the mirror, I**
    a) **smile proudly**
    b) **laugh and cry hysterically**
    c) **don't see anything**

10. **To me, sex feels like**
    a) **a pleasant way to spend twenty minutes**
    b) **a religious experience**
    c) **dozens of scorpions crawling on my skin trying to sting and pinch my genitals**

ANSWERS:

1—c; 2—c; 3—c; 4—a or b; 5—d; 6—c; 7—a; 8—a; 9—b; 10—b or c.

If you scored seven or more correct answers, you're well on your way to asexuality and you'll never have to worry about scoring again.

DIVERSIONS WHEN YOU'RE IN THE MOOD FOR SEX

Scientists believe that the most important sex organ is not in your boxers or panties but in your head—the human brain. If you are to successfully not engage in sexual intercourse—which certainly must be a goal of yours since you're reading this book and not out looking for sex—you must distract your mind from the surge of hormones and the rush of blood to your genitals. One common diversion is pain: slam a car door on your pinky, have a full body-wax, have root canal work, or sit on a rake. These methods are most reliable.

However, less extreme diversions exist. Diligent researchers went for months without sex to bring you the following recommendations.

1. Organize the food in your refrigerator alphabetically.

2. Make a copy of everything you throw away.

3. Crochet your own coffee filters.

4. Try to balance the federal budget without the aid of a calculator.

5. Change all the shoelaces in your shoes.

6. Redecorate the fishtank.

7. Visit relatives you thought had died.

8. Clean the hair out of the drain.

9. Scale and gut a fish.

10. Take pictures of your underwear.

11. Try to remember everything Reagan forgot.

QUESTION:

**What would you substitute
for sex?**

ANSWER:

Marriage.

GAYLE SILVERMAN
philosopher

VOLUNTEER YOUR SERVICES

▲ Nothing numbs gonads like a little selfless, sexless community service. The list of people and organizations who want to suck your time, energy, and lifeblood for free is endless. Here are some very helpful organizations that could use your volunteer services. No matter whom you were fantasizing about, you'll stop thinking about sex as soon as you step into an apartment that hasn't been cleaned since the Gulf of Tonkin Resolution to pick up someone's dirty laundry. Or you could donate blood to the Red Cross. After giving blood, don't just lie there to recover— jump up and use the resulting dizziness, nausea, and fatigue in your efforts not to have sex. If you feel fine and are thinking about sex, give another pint.

Old Newsboy Goodfellow Fund of Detroit
P.O. Box 32702
Detroit, MI 48232

A local group made up of former newspaper carriers. Old newsboys hawk papers on one day each year and the profits are used to make Christmas better for needy children. No conventions, no publications.

International Sunshine Society
105 Marsh Road
Wilmington, DE 19809

A philanthropic organization founded in 1896, this group has an annual convention and publishes the *Sunshine Bulletin*.

Drifters, Inc.
7947 Glenside Place
University City, MO 63130

Women dedicated to improving lives of black Americans and raising the aspirations of young blacks. Founded in 1954, the group has annual conventions and publishes *Jus' Driftin'*.

Servants in Faith and Technology
Rt. 1, Box D-14
Lineville, AL 36266

Churches, church groups, and Christian individuals concerned with development through the use of appropriate technology. Objective is to enable people to meet their own needs.

Also consider volunteering for:

Sleep experiments

Psychological testing

Dermatological testing

Crash-dummy work

Recording books for the blind—but omit all erotic passages

American leprosy missions

TOLL-FREE PHONE NUMBERS TO CALL

▲ Though the telephone has become an instrument of sex, it is now an even more valuable tool in the heroic efforts *not* to have sex. This does not mean calling your Uncle Louie when you're in the mood for sex and asking if the doctor lanced that boil that was bothering him. That sort of conversation is dangerous. Not only will it be too brief to completely distract you, but the very nature of such calls—the tedious focus on relationships, sickness, and mortality—will send you fleeing out into the night to have sex with any human, animal, or vegetable to reaffirm your physical vitality. So don't call Uncle Louie.

The phone calls you make must divert you for hours on end, up to and including entire weekends. It is critical that the calls be interesting, informative, nonarousing, and cheap. Only toll-free numbers can give you all these things at once. There are about 450,000 listings of 800 numbers. Just dial 800-555-1212 for directory assistance and wave bye-bye to thoughts about sex. Take a look at what Saturday night has in store for you.

Toll-Free Numbers:

Acne Health Care Centers International, 800-235-2263; 800-225-2263

Alpo, 800-241-2567

American Mathematical Society, 800-556-7774

American Medical Radio News, 800-621-8094

Asbestos Technical Information Service, 800-334-8571, ext. 6741

Beech-Nut Nutrition Hotline, 800-523-6633; 800-492-2384

Butterball Turkey Talkline, 800-323-4848

Clairol Hotline, 800-223-5800

Conservation and Renewable Energy Inquiry and Referral Service (CAREIRS), 800-523-2929; 800-462-4983; 800-233-3071

Cuisinart Hotline, 800-243-8540

Dale Carnegie, 800-231-5800; 800-392-2424

Dial-a-Plumber "Plumber's Hotline," 800-521-7488; 800-572-5398

Economic Statistics Hotline, 800-424-7964; Washington, D.C.: 800-488-8358

Ho Ho Hotline, 800-458-4646

Life and Health Insurance Information Hotline, 800-423-8000

Loctite Hotline—Automotive and Consumer Group, 800-321-9188

Major Appliance Consumer Action Panel (MACAP), 800-621-0477

Meat and Poultry Hotline, 800-535-4555

Mentor Contraceptives, 800-435-3555

National Appropriate Technology Assistance Service (NATAS), 800-428-2525; 800-428-1718

Nutrition Hotline, 800-222-6325

Pillsbury Consumer Hotline, 800-328-4466

RCRA/Superfund Hotline, 800-424-9346

Scott Lawn Hotline, 800-543-8873; 800-762-4010

Second Opinion on Non-Emergency Surgery, 800-638-6833; MD: 800-492-6603

Tele-Tax, 800-554-4477

Venereal Disease Hotline, 800-227-8922;
CA: 800-982-5883

White House News, 800-424-9090

WHEN AND HOW TO GET FREE THINGS

▲ Few things in life are as diverting as a surprise in the mail. Certainly you deserve *something*—you're not having sex, dinners out, or fun. Rewarding yourself is psychologically sound. But, as always, money enters into it. Since you can't run up an enormous tab at Tiffany's and you crave something that'll provide more distraction than an antique digital grandfather clock or a pictorial survey of Bauhaus soup spoons, what can you do? The answer is as near as your mailbox and it's *free*. You can send away for literally thousands of free items advertised in magazines and newspapers. And most of these items will improve your mind while shriveling your desires. Don't let anyone tell you "nothing's free."

FREE THINGS TO SEND AWAY FOR

Stain Removal Guide
Maytag Company
Consumer Education Department
Newton, IA 50208

An easy-to-follow chart with specific laundering directions for just about any spill imaginable.

Welcome the Birds
 Rubbermaid Specialty Products, Inc.
 Statesville, NC 28677

How-tos for attracting birds to your yard and keeping them well fed.

Discover the Pleasures of Roses
Send stamped, self-addressed envelope to:
 American Rose Society
 Box 3000
 Shreveport, LA 71130

Helps you start a garden and keep it growing.

How to Get and Keep the Right Job
 Carnation Company, Public Relations
 Carnation Building
 5045 Wilshire Boulevard
 Los Angeles, CA 90036

Interview dos and don'ts, plus on-the-job performance pointers in this booklet.

Hassle-Free Cleaning for Singles and Other Busy People
 Johnson Wax Consumer Services Center
 1525 Howe Street
 Racine, WI 53403

Includes a section on how to make the bed while you're still in it.

New Room in Your Kitchen
 Rubbermaid, Inc.
 Home Service Center
 Wooster, OH 44691

Identifies common space problems, offers simple solutions. Cutouts and pasteups help you redesign your space.

Heart Facts
> **The American Heart Association**
> National Center
> 7320 Greenville Avenue
> Dallas, TX 75231

Roughly half of all deaths are associated with heart disease. Learn more about this crucial organ.

Quick Answers to Commonly Asked
Questions About Food
> **Institute of Food Technologists**
> 221 N. La Salle Street
> Chicago, IL 60601

Discusses vegetarianism, nitrites, even Chinese-restaurant syndrome, among other topics.

New York Stock Exchange Glossary
> **NYSE**
> 11 Wall Street
> New York, NY 10005

Maybe this glossary, which explains everything from accrued interest to zero coupon bonds, will help.

How to Read a Financial Report
> **Merrill Lynch**
> The Blueprint Program
> New Brunswick, NJ 08989-0412

Hard to understand, requires several readings to comprehend.

Nutrition Health Review
> **American Parade of Catalogs**
> 144 S. First Street
> Dept. 471296
> P.O. Box 4507
> Burbank, CA 91503

Send for a sample copy of *Nutrition Health Review*, a consumer's medical journal, packed with the latest news of health, fitness, and diets.

JOIN A GROUP

▲ You are not alone. Millions of other Americans are also turning their backs on sex. How do you overcome the tidal wave of hormones that we all face upon sexual arousal? People band together in groups. In unity there is strength—and hopefully, not many erections. The following list is chock-full of groups that you can join to avoid sexual intercourse. Join them and get right into the swing of things by volunteering for a committee or offering to be parliamentarian. And trying to figure out how you got into all this will also divert your mind from you-know-what.

GROUPS TO BELONG TO

The Society for the Preservation and Encouragement of Barbershop Singing in America
6135 Third Avenue
Kenosha, WI 53141

Founded in 1938, the society aims to preserve and encourage the barbershop style of singing and to live in harmony with its fellow men. Another of its goals is to "Keep America Singing" with "Songs of Service." And to promote hot towels.

The Federation of Historical Bottle Clubs
c/o Gene Bradberry
4098 Faxon Avenue
Memphis, TN 38122

Founded in 1969, the federation wants to "promote, foster, and encourage all activities toward the betterment of bottle collecting."

National Button Society
Box 116
Lamoni, IA 50140

Since 1938, the society has worked to "preserve for future generations all that is beautiful and historic in buttons." Keep an eye out for the national convention.

International Flat Earth Research Society
P.O. Box 2533
Lancaster, CA 93534

Founded in 1800, and dedicated to establishing "as a fact that this earth is flat and plane and that it does not spin and whirl one thousand miles an hour and to expose modern astronomical science as a fraud, myth, a false religion."

Jim Smith Society
2016 Milltown
Camp Hill, PA 17011

Not open to just anyone named Smith—only Jims. Founded in 1969.

North American Trail Complex
307 S. Highland
P. O. Box 805
Bloomington, IN 47401

Organized to develop a vast network of hiking trails to interconnect all regions of the continent. It needs "volunteer scouts"—no experience needed—to explore trails and determine their desirability and conditions.

Procrastinators' Club of America
1111 Broad-Locust Building
Philadelphia, PA 19102

Holds irregular and late meetings. Founded in 1956, its membership protested the War of 1812, and went to Spain to raise money for three ships with which to discover America.

Chili USA
c/o R. N. Dunganan
1919 Pennsylvania Avenue, N.W.
Washington, D.C. 20006

Members are putting heat on Congress to designate chili as America's national food.

National Puzzlers' League
299 McCall Road
Rochester, NY 14616

Devoted since 1883 to the fun of word puzzling, "a pastime which will give you more pleasure, for less expense, than any other hobby under the sun."

Richard III Society, Inc.
9 Weld Street, Apt. 48
Framingham, MA 01701

Looks at the fifteenth century in light of recent research and attempts to tell the truth about Richard III and to dispel Shakespeare's version.

Thoreau Society, Inc.
State University College
Genesee, NY 14454

An informal organization of students and followers of the life and writings of Henry David Thoreau. Publishes a quarterly that reprints rare Thoreauviana. Founded in 1941.

**Stone Skipping and Gerplunking Club of
Mackinac Island Unicorns, Ltd., Conglomerate**
Lake Superior State College
Sault Ste. Marie, MI 49783

Founded in 1969 to "encourage development of the sport of stone skipping." Tournament every year—current world record is eighteen skips established in 1936 (prior to formal competition).

The International Wizard of Oz Club
220 N. Eleventh Street
Escanaba, MI 49829

Founded in 1957 to "promote reading and collecting of the writings of L. Frank Baum and his associates and successors in Oz." Publishes *Oziana*, which contains stories, poems, and artwork by club members.

CASH REWARDS

▲ What's on your mind more than sex? *Money*. And that's the way it should be. You simply need to build on this natural inclination to avoid sex.

Begin by looking at everything in your life in terms of money—assign monetary values to your friends, relatives, co-workers, religious beliefs, and personal values. For instance, you might price your parents at $2,500, your best friend at $100,000, your belief in God at $1.25, and your personal integrity at $1.6 million. Constantly focus your thoughts on money. Instead of just conducting a common conversation with your best friend, try calculating his or her worth in yen, deutsche marks, and pounds sterling.

After time passes, you may find it no longer satisfying simply to play with these great sums in your head. You must lay your hands on some real money. This is simple. Win the Publisher's Clearing House Sweepstakes. Or, better yet, try for one of these terrific cash rewards. They're yours for the taking. Never forget—*money*.

SIX CASH REWARDS THAT YOU COULD WIN

1. **For bald-eagle killers.** The Illinois Wildlife Federation will pay $500 for information leading to the arrest and conviction of anyone who has killed a bald eagle in Illinois. To claim reward, contact: Illinois Wildlife Federation, 13005 Western Avenue, Blue Island, IL 60406.

2. **For the remains of Bigfoot.** Project Bigfoot in Seattle, Washington, has offered a $1,000 reward for any identifiable remains, such as the skull, teeth, or bones, of a Bigfoot. Local residents have reported seeing the seven-foot, four-hundred-pound creature over the last 160 years but no reward has ever been collected. Contact: Project Bigfoot, P. O. Box 444, North Gate Station, Seattle, WA 98125.

3. **For delivery for enemy weaponry.** The People's Republic of China offers up to $4 million in gold for Taiwanese military craft and weaponry. The $4 million is for a destroyer; $2 million for a submarine; $1.4 million for an F-5E jet; $14,000 for a C-47 plane. Taiwan offers similar rewards. Contact: People's Republic of China Liaison Office, 2300 Connecticut Avenue, Washington, D.C. 20008, or Government Information Office, 3 Chung Hsiao East Road, Section 1, Taipei, Taiwan 100, People's Republic of China.

4. **For information leading to the indictment of bank robbers.** The Washington State Bankers Association offers an award for information leading to the arrest and indictment of a bank robber. Bank employees and law enforcement officials are not eligible. Contact: Washington State Bankers Association, 1218 Third Avenue, Suite 505, Seattle, WA 98101.

5. **For the capture of a UFO.** Cutty Sark, the whiskey manufacturer, offers one million pounds for the capture of a spaceship or other vehicle that the Science Museum of London can certify as having come from outer space. The British Unidentified Flying Object Research Association advises that the chances of collecting the reward

are nil. Contact: Cutty Sark, 3 St. James Street, London, SW1, England.

6. **For a world chess champion computer.** The Fredkin Charitable Foundation of Boston, MA, offers a $100,000 reward for the first computer program to defeat the world chess champion.

FASTING

▲ Many of you may confuse food and eating with love and sex. Lucky you. If you can convince yourself that food *is* sex, that's all you need to live a fulfilling, chunky, sex-free life. But for the rest of you, who know the difference between strudel and *schtupping*, you must force food to take the superior position. You must make food the central issue of your life. In order to do this, you must stop eating—and fast. Fasting will make you more deeply obsessed about food than you could ever imagine. At the end of a four-day fast, you'll shove your way past dozens of horny men or pleading virgins to get to a bowl of Cocoa Puffs with milk. And you won't stop eating until you're stuffed and bloated, lost in a carbohydrate stupor—in no shape for sex. By the time you're coherent again, you've gained so much weight no one would have sex with you anyway, so—you guessed it—time to fast again. Then that lovely binge. Then a fast. Binge. Fast. Binge. Fast. Do you see a pattern emerging? Your life will soon revolve around food, either the pangs and fevers of not having any or the luxurious discomfort of gluttony. The following fasts are heartily recommended:

WATER FAST

BREAKFAST	LUNCH	DINNER	SNACK
8 oz. water	8 oz. water	12 oz. water	2⅓ oz. water

You can apply the same portions to these fasts as well:

Juice fast

Bouillon fast

Diet Coke fast

Distilled water fast

Reconstituted lemon juice fast

Olive oil fast

THE TRIATHLON

▲ If you are truly serious about not having sex, you need a truly serious diversion. There is only one. The triathlon. It demands a year of training, during which you must spend a minimum of six hours per day swimming in the ocean, cycling, and running. Add that to eight hours each for work and sleep, an hour for eating, commuting, and TV, a half hour for working the knots out of your muscles, and another half hour to shave your chest and legs (required for swimming), and you can see that the time you'll have for sex—or even to think about it—is zip.

Triathlon training has several benefits that no other diversion can offer. First, it gets you into top physical condition. This will add years to your life—long, sexless years. Second, throngs of adoring fans will worship you as you compete, but expect absolutely nothing of you sexually because you're totally wasted. And third, after a sex-free life of triathlon competition, you'll have rooms full of commemorative T-shirts and trophies, no groupies, and a guilt-free existence.

ADDITIONAL BENEFITS OF TRIATHLONS

1. Heat exhaustion

2. Heat cramps

3. Heat stroke (indicated by vomiting, diarrhea, and death)

4. Destroys knees and relationships

5. Kinesiologists estimate that 97 percent of relationships will automatically break up due to triathlons

TRAINING TIPS

In order to derive the most from your training, always work out when:

> **The temperature is ninety degrees or higher**
>
> **There's no wind**
>
> **The humidity is 90 percent or higher**

BE A HERO—PUSH YOURSELF!

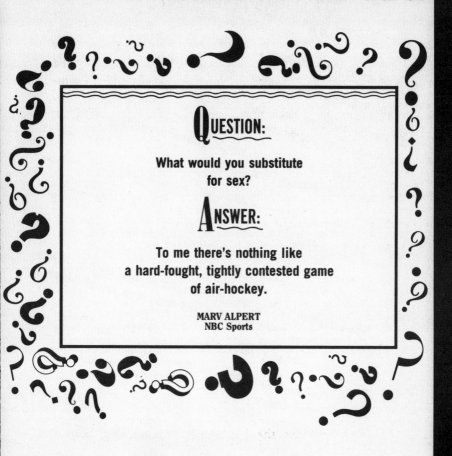

QUESTION:

What would you substitute
for sex?

ANSWER:

To me there's nothing like
a hard-fought, tightly contested game
of air-hockey.

MARV ALPERT
NBC Sports

DIVERSION SUMMARY

▲ If you follow the preceding tips and guidelines, you should have no trouble being diverted from sexual intercourse. As a matter of fact, if you throw yourself into these activities with enough enthusiasm, you'll even forget what it was you wanted to be diverted from. Now that you've finished this chapter, it's time to evaluate what you've learned. Fill out this questionnaire and see how you rate.

QUESTIONNAIRE

1. I never again want to have sex with_____.

2. The volunteer organization I most admire is_____.

3. I've worked so hard this year I've received _____ promotions and salary increases.

4. I've learned so many worthwhile and uplifting things from 800 numbers including:_____

_____ and_____

5. After running my first triathlon, I'll feel _____ about not having sex.

6. I believe fasting and thinking about food all the time is _____ and the perfect diversion from you-know-what.

_____ me.

7. My parents never _____

8. The most fulfilling part of my life is my _____ club/group and I'm chairperson of our annual _____ Weekend Jubilee.

9. Now that I've found a spiritual life through the _____ religious order, God tells me to _____

_____

_____

You can judge for yourself by the ease and thoroughness with which you are able to fill out this questionnaire just how well you're diverting yourself. If you stumbled on several of the questions or became aroused upon just seeing the word *sex*, you need additional guidance.

SUBSTITUTES

Some of you may have experienced sex on a deeper level than those shallow people who were easily distracted by the diversions presented in the previous chapter. For you, intercourse is a thundering passion in your belly, a quivering ache that only primitive, plunging, soul-shattering bangity-bangity-bang can assuage. Pleasure rips through your muscles like a hurricane, you cry out, but no sound is heard above the roar of your blood and the groans and cries of the storm of passion. Sex is all. Nothing else will do. Except . . . well, remember that time with the brunette in Chicago? The pizza afterward *was* better than she was. And what about the broker in San Francisco? That stock tip he gave was better than he'll ever be in bed. The lesson here is that some things are as good as, if not better than, sex. Whenever possible, use such a substitute to deflect your inclination toward humping. Sexual substitutes are all over the place. Go out, pick one up, take it home with you, then settle in for a nice evening of something that feels as good as sex, but without the risk.

EXPERIENCES THAT ARE BETTER THAN SEX

▲ In the waning months of the Nixon administration, a special report came briefly to light and then disappeared. It stated that a few, select experiences were actually *better* than sex. Ample research data was provided as proof. Nixon swiftly ordered the report sealed and marked "National Security" shortly after he made his "I am not a crook" speech. He tried to conceal this information, apparently fearing a population constantly coming to a sort of "orgasm" via these experiences, while he was stuck experiencing the preliminaries of impeachment.

The Freedom of Information Act, however, has made knowledge of these secret experiences available to all Americans. Thousands of experiences were tested, yet only those listed below brought a pleasure greater than sexual intercourse. You might think that being given a new Porsche for free would be better than sex, but scientifically, it simply wasn't. It rated below getting to meet Johnny Carson.

The following are experiences that rate high:

1. Getting a great haircut.

2. Having your shoes dyed to match—and they match.

3. Finding the perfect apartment—and it's rent controlled.

4. Getting your shirts back from the laundry and none of the buttons are broken.

5. Going to a department store and finding the only thing you like is on sale.

6. Getting sick and discovering your health insurance covers everything.

7. Balancing your checkbook and finding a thousand-dollar error in your favor.

9. Your parents forget to call on Sunday—and you never hear from them again.

10. Being called in by your boss and being told that you are indispensable to the company and you're getting a raise—retroactively.

11. A waiter telling you you overtipped.

12. The discovery of a pill that makes everything you eat noncaloric.

FOOD AND EATING: BETTER-THAN-SEX RECIPES

▲ Eating. Does it seem too obvious? In your pursuit of the perfect substitute for sex, nothing is too obvious. Eat food, live food, breathe food, and your life—as well as you—will be too full for anything even remotely resembling sex. You can develop a taste for specific foods to substitute for your favorite sexual acts; when a desire for a certain type of sex overwhelms you, simply consume the food that you've come to associate with that act. A noted sex expert and gourmet suggests these substitutions:

Intercourse, missionary position—
1 Snickers bar

Intercourse, woman on top—
1 Hostess Snoball

Intercourse, rear entry—
Van De Kamp's Batter-Dipped French-Fried
Fish Kabobs

Fellatio—
1 Hebrew National kosher hot dog

Cunnilingus—
Winchell's vanilla doughnut holes

Sodomy—
Del Monte's canned burritos

A simple rule of thumb is eat as much and as often as you can. When in doubt, eat. You will soon discover that there are many foods that can be as good as sex and the only protection you'll need is a napkin. Before reading any further, take a break and go fix yourself a hot fudge sundae. Embrace it, explore it, finish it quickly. Delicious, huh? Add to the incredible oral pleasure you've just enjoyed the comfort of knowing (1) the ice cream wasn't carrying any sexually transmitted diseases, and (2) you didn't have to wait for the ice cream to finish first, and you will start to see the advantages of food over sex.

DEEP LUST PIE

▼

SERVES 10 TO 12

COOKIE CRUST

½ cup (1 stick) unsalted butter

2 cups graham cracker crumbs

2 cups gingersnap cookie crumbs

⅔ to ¾ cup cold milk

½ cup mini-chocolate chips

MOCHA CREAM

2 cups whipping cream

1½ cups sugar

2 tablespoons cold, strong espresso coffee

1 package (8 ounces) semisweet chocolate squares

6 large egg whites at room temperature

½ cup mini-chocolate chips

In 2-quart saucepan, melt butter over low heat. Remove from heat. Stir in graham cracker crumbs and gingersnap crumbs until well mixed. Add milk while tossing with a fork until the crumbs are moistened. Stir in ½ cup mini-chocolate chips. Lightly press crumb mixture on bottom and three-fourths up sides of 10-inch springform pan. Refrigerate 2 hours.

In small bowl, with electric mixer, beat whipping cream until foamy. Gradually beat in ½ cup sugar until stiff peaks form. With a spatula or wire whisk, gently fold in espresso.

In heavy 1-quart saucepan, melt chocolate squares over low heat until smooth, stirring constantly. Let cool to room temperature.

In large bowl, with electric mixer, beat egg whites until soft peaks form. Gradually beat in ¾ cup sugar until stiff peaks form. With spatula or wire whisk, gently fold cooled melted chocolate into beaten egg whites, and set aside.

Fold whipped cream into chocolate mixture. Pour mixture into cookie crust. Chill 2 hours.

Sprinkle remaining chocolate chips on top of dessert. Freeze for 6 hours or overnight. To serve, run a small metal spatula around the side of the dessert to loosen from the pan. Remove side of springform pan. You may want to thaw it for 30 minutes before you cut it.

THROBBING PEARS WITH RASPBERRY PUREE

SERVES 4

1½ cups sugar

1½ cups water

4 ripe, firm Bosc or Bartlett pears

½ lemon or lemon juice

1 package (10 ounces) frozen raspberries, thawed

1 tablespoon sugar

1 tablespoon cornstarch

2 tablespoons cold water

¼ cup raspberry liqueur

Blanched slivered almonds

In a 4-quart saucepan, combine sugar and water. Heat to boiling, stirring until sugar dissolves. Meanwhile, peel each pear; cut in half lengthwise and remove core with a melon baller. Immediately rub pears gently with the cut side of lemon or brush them with lemon juice to prevent discoloration.

Gently slide pears into simmering sugar syrup. Simmer for 10 minutes, or until pears are just tender. Drain pears; cool; cover and refrigerate until cold.

In 1-quart saucepan, combine raspberries and sugar. In cup, mix cornstarch and water; stir into raspberries. Heat mixture to boiling, stirring constantly, until thickened. Simmer 1 minute. Remove from heat and mash raspberry mixture through a sieve into a small bowl; discard seeds. Stir raspberry liqueur into puree. Cover and refrigerate until cold.

For each serving, place 2 pear halves in a dish. Spoon raspberry puree over the pear and sprinkle with almonds.

ESTHER SHEAR'S
(NEW YORK'S BEST SEPHARDIC CATERER) BETTER-THAN-SEX CHOCOLATE COOKIES

▼

MAKES APPROXIMATELY 40 COOKIES

8 *ounces semisweet chocolate*	2 *eggs*
3 *tablespoons margarine (sweet)*	¾ *cup sugar*
⅓ *cup sifted flour*	2 *tablespoons powdered instant coffee*
¼ *teaspoon baking powder*	2 *cups walnuts and hazelnuts, broken in small pieces*
Pinch of salt	1 *cup chocolate chips*

Melt semisweet chocolate with margarine in double boiler; set aside and cool.

Sift together flour, baking powder, and salt. Set aside.

In a small bowl, beat eggs and sugar at high speed for a few minutes. Then add cooled chocolate. With a rubber spatula, add the flour mixture until well blended. Then add nuts, chocolate chips, and powdered instant coffee.

Drop by teaspoonsful on a foil-covered pan and bake for 8 to 10 minutes at 350 degrees. Let cool before removing from foil.

CHOCOLATE SLAVE CAKE

SERVES 8

16 **ounces semisweet chocolate**

½ **cup (1 stick) unsalted butter**

1½ **teaspoons all purpose flour**

1½ **teaspoons sugar**

1 **teaspoon hot water**

4 **eggs, separated**

1 **cup whipping cream**

Preheat oven to 425 degrees. Grease bottom of 8-inch springform pan. Melt chocolate and butter in top of double boiler. Add flour, sugar, and water, and blend well. Add egg yolks one at a time, beating well after each addition. Beat egg whites until stiff but not dry. Fold into chocolate mixture. Turn into pan and bake 15 minutes *only*; cake will look very uncooked in center. Let cake cool completely (as cake cools, it will sink a bit in the middle), then chill or freeze.

Whip cream until soft peaks form. Spread very thick layer over top of cake, smoothing with a spatula. Cut cake while cold, but let stand at room temperature about 15 minutes before serving.

If the preceding recipes don't capture your heart and sexual appetite, try devoting yourself to one that takes *two complete days* to prepare. By the time you're done, you'll be too tired to eat, let alone have sex.

CONFIT D'OIE
(PRESERVED GOOSE)

Bleed a fat goose, pluck, singe, then completely cool it. Slit the goose down the back from neck to tail. Draw it carefully to avoid harming the liver, which can be used in cooking other dishes.

Remove the fat that surrounds the gizzard and the intestines.

Cut the goose into four pieces: the two breast pieces with the wings attached and the two legs. Leave the carcass bones attached to each quarter.

Rub the goose pieces inside and out with spiced salt. To make spiced salt, combine 2 pounds sea salt, finely crushed, 1 pound sugar, 4 cloves, 1 bay leaf, and 1 sprig of thyme, crushed to a powder. A large handful of this salt is enough for one goose.

After rubbing the goose with salt, put the pieces in a glazed bowl and cover with the remaining spiced salt and a dishcloth. Let marinate in this brine for at least 24 hours.

Then remove the pieces of goose, shake the salt off them, and carefully wipe. Plunge the goose into a saucepan filled with tepid melted fat—half goose fat from the bird and half pork fat, both clarified and strained.

Gradually bring to a slow boil. The fat should boil but not smoke. At the start of the cooking the fat will be cloudy, but as the goose cooks, it will get clearer. It takes 2 hours to produce a perfect confit. The goose will be cooked when the fat is clear; if it has been cooked very slowly, a needle should penetrate the meat easily.

Drain the pieces of goose and remove any loose bones from the carcass or the legs.

Using a glazed earthenware pot, pour in a layer of the cooking fat. Let it harden; then place the goose meat on top, without letting it touch the sides of the pot, in a single layer. Cover with another layer of half-congealed fat. Repeat until all the goose meat is covered.

Two days later pour a new layer of hot fat into the pot to fill any empty spaces. The following day pour on the surface a last layer of pure pork fat, well cooked, which in turn will harden.

Cut a piece of wax paper the size of the pot and place it on top of the fat.

Cover the pot and keep the confit d'oie in a dry, cool place or refrigerate.

Each time you want to use a piece of confit, first remove the pork fat, then the cooking fat. After you remove a piece of goose, first replace the goose fat, then the pork fat. This way, the confit can be kept for a whole season.

QUESTION:

What would you substitute for sex?

ANSWER:

Eating.

BELINDA CARLISLE
recording artist

THINGS TO THINK ABOUT BEFORE HAVING SEX

▲ She's begging you, "Now! Now!" You're about to proceed when you suddenly remember, *Oh, my God! I'm not supposed to be having sex!* What can you do? You need an effective mental system to produce instant impotence—the only believable excuse for not having intercourse. Use these thoughts in an emergency, like smelling salts, to wake you and save you from sexual ruin. To help you memorize them, they've been arranged so that the first letters of the words spell out your goal:

L atest VISA bill—the amount and due date

I magine a bowling ball slamming into your groin

M ental image: your parents doing it

P regnant—she could get pregnant

D imensions—it's too small

I magine that you can't get it up

C ircumcision—the pain

K ol Nidre

SHOPPING AND MALL FACTS

▲ Many people complain that shopping is just too shallow a substitute for sex. Pay them no heed. You must do what is right for you. And if shopping is the most satisfying substitute of all the ones offered in this book, then grab it and take it—yes, take it, take it now, with all the force of your being, lunging in and out, in and out of stores, sucking on bargains, whipping out your charge cards, squeezing the last ounce of shopping out of yourself, as you moan under the weight of your purchases, until you cry with ecstasy and collapse as you enter Neiman-Marcus. Was it good for you?

SHOPPING QUIZ: ARE YOU A GOOD SHOPPER?

1. **When shopping, I**
   a) buy things I don't really need
   b) look for and buy only bargains
   c) shove others out of the way to get to what I want

2. **I consider it a good shopping day only if I**
   a) go $250 over my credit limit on all my charge cards
   b) come home with something I'm really happy with
   c) shove others out of the way to get to what I want

3. **For shopping advice, I rely on**
   a) friends
   b) advertisements
   c) religious visions

4. **Salespeople treat me like**
   a) Donald Trump
   b) a large, molelike creature
   c) a small, molelike creature

5. **At my favorite stores, I**
   a) know the sales clerks by name
   b) shoplift
   c) sleep with the clerks to find out when the next sale is
   d) shove others out of the way to get to what I want

ANSWERS:

There are no correct answers to this quiz.

MALL FACTS—A PSYCHOLOGICAL AID

- The word *mall* is an Old English word that meant a strip of lawn where a croquetlike game called pall-mall was played.

- Seventy percent of the adult population shops at regional malls more than three times a month.

- People stay for an average of eighty minutes each time they visit a mall.

- Eighty-six percent of shoppers buy something to eat while at the mall.

- Teenagers spend an average of $25.96 on each trip to the mall. And they visit an average of 3.5 stores per trip.

- There are so many shoe stores in malls because mall owners are aware that the average woman buys six pairs of shoes a year.

- Malls in America earn a combined income of about $300 billion a year.

- Across the nation there are more than 30,000 off-price outlet malls where you can save from 30 to 80 percent on name-brand goods.

$\mathbf{D}$EVELOP A PHOBIA

▲ A sure way to keep you from enjoying or even participating in sex is to develop a phobia. Not an easy one like acrophobia (fear of heights) or thanatophobia (fear of death)— these are commonplace and don't provide enough distraction. Any Tom, Dick, or Jane can have these and still have a knockout sex life. And it must be an emotionally charged fear—not, say, of plants (botanophobia) or of words (verbophobia), nor should it be too complex like arachibutyrophobia, the fear of getting peanut butter stuck in the roof of your mouth. With a fear that obscure, someone is bound to get hurt and some psychiatrist is bound to get rich. A nice, simple, debilitating dread that directly relates to sex is recommended. Any of the following phobias will do just fine.

$\mathbf{P}$HOBIAS TO DEVELOP

AICHMOPHOBIA—a morbid fear of pointed objects, including penises and penis symbols

ANDROPHOBIA—an intense, pathologic fear of men

ANTHROPOPHOBIA—a fear of people

AUTOMYSOPHOBIA—a morbid, neurotic fear of being dirty or smelling unclean

BACILLOPHOBIA—a fear of microbes

CLINOPHOBIA—a fear of beds

COITOPHOBIA—a morbid fear of sexual intercourse

CYPRIDOPHOBIA—an intense, morbid fear of contracting VD

EUROTOPHOBIA—a morbid fear of the female genital organs

GAMOPHOBIA—an intense, morbid fear of marriage

GENOPHOBIA—an intense, morbid fear of sex

GYMNOPHOBIA—a morbid fear of naked bodies

GYNEPHOBIA—a fear of women

HAPTEPHOBIA—a morbid fear of being touched

HEDONOPHOBIA—a morbid fear of experiencing pleasure of any kind

MAIEUSIOPHOBIA—an intense, morbid fear of childbirth

MYSOPHOBIA—fear of germs or contamination

PANTOPHOBIA—fear of fears

PATHOPHOBIA—fear of disease

PORNOPHOBIA—fear of prostitutes

TRICHOPHOBIA—fear of hair

XENOPHOBIA—fear of strangers

PET OBSESSIONS

▲ This is a nation obsessed with sex. Advertisers use sex to sell everything from booze to computers—everything except pet food. When was the last time a commercial for Purina Gravy Chow left you thinking about sex? You should answer "never," unless you're a very sick individual. Take a clue from this phenomenon and get a pet. Not a Baggie filled with half-dead goldfish or a couple of flea-bitten gerbils. Find yourself a real pet—a cat, a dog, a carnivorous bird—that you can teach a stupid trick to, buy expensive, pointless gifts for, and become so obsessed with that your friends will think you've lost it. They're right. What you've lost, however, isn't your mind, but something much better—any time for or inclination toward having sex.

As with any obsession, begin slowly. Start by spending a day or two looking through name books before you name your new baby. Once you have that, you can order all the personalized food dishes, toys, and clothing with your pet's name on them. Before you know it, you'll be planning social events around your pet's bowel habits, insisting he/she be in every photo taken of you, and declining the perfect date because you have to sit with your pet through the more violent parts of *The Love Connection*. Don't forget the added bonus—pets last longer than most relationships. So, go get a pet, open your checkbook, and kiss sex good-bye.

JOIN A RELIGIOUS GROUP

▲ Give up sex and find God. Channeling all your sexual energy into a newfound religion and then trying to convert everyone you happen to bump into is the safest use of the missionary position. This substitute has a hidden bonus: no one can say for certain that Heaven exists, but if it does you've got a better shot at it than some poor stiff who's still humping his brains out.

THE SERVANTS OF THE GOOD SHEPHERD

Become a priest—the easy way. Nontraditional method leaves type and location of assignment mostly up to you. Unnecessary to relocate or abandon present career. Celibacy optional.

> **The Servants of the Good Shepherd**
> 1529 Pleasant Valley Boulevard
> Altoona, PA 16602

ECKANKAR

Located in Las Vegas, this Hindu group with twenty thousand members was founded by U.S. soldier of fortune Paul Twitchell who claimed a five-hundred-year-old Tibetan guru educated him in the feat of "soul travel"—the ability to travel anywhere with your mind while still sitting at home. Members also believe in reincarnation.

> **Eckankar**
> 1514 South Maryland Park
> Las Vegas, NV 89104

NICHIREN SHOSHU

This Buddhist cult, based on the wisdom of a thirteenth-century monk named Nichiren, believes that if you chant you can get anything in the world that you desire. The all-powerful chant is "Nam-myoho-rengekyo." Call your local Buddhist temple to find the chapter nearest you: look under "churches" in the Yellow Pages.

BODY OF CHRIST

Known as "The Garbage Eaters," this nomadic cult of fifty or sixty members wanders around the country and survives by eating out of dumpsters behind fast-food restaurants. Their leader is known as Brother Evangelist and says God speaks through him.

Females who join are required to always look toward the ground and whisper whenever they speak to a man. Women must also carry dirt in their pockets as a constant reminder of how low they are.

To find them, hang around dumpsters behind fast-food restaurants.

ATHLETES IN ACTION

Athletic ministry of Campus Crusade for Christ. Seeks to present the claims of Jesus Christ throughout the world and to win, build, and send men for Him through the platform of sports.

> **Athletes in Action**
> 4790 Irvine Boulevard #105-325
> Irvine, CA 92714

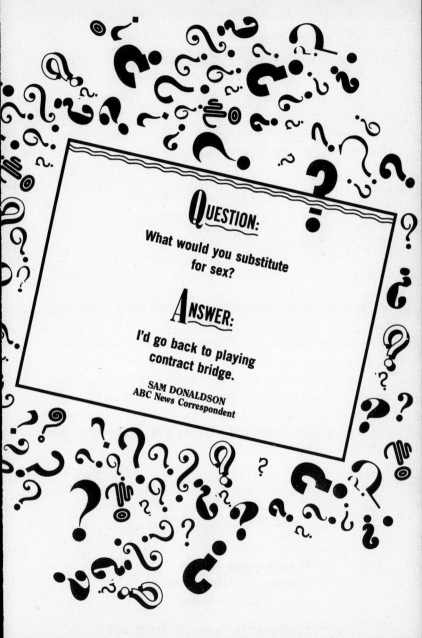

QUESTION:

What would you substitute
for sex?

ANSWER:

I'd go back to playing
contract bridge.

SAM DONALDSON
ABC News Correspondent

MASTURBATION

Hey, don't knock masturbation.
It's sex with someone
I love.

WOODY ALLEN *Annie Hall*, 1977

▲ The most elementary, primal substitute has been left for last. When you've tried everything else in vain and you throw up your hands, isn't it lucky they usually land in your lap? It's nature's way of saying, "Go ahead! No one's looking."

Masturbation has brought so much pleasure to so many people and made so many magazines soggy and unreadable, that to describe techniques or positions seems superfluous. Know the pros and cons and soon you'll be eating out of the palm of your hand.

The only reason I feel guilty about
masturbation is because I
do it so badly.

DAVID STEINBERG *The Tonight Show* NBC-TV, 1972

Masturbation: Benefits Of

1. Inexpensive
2. You can operate heavy machinery afterward
3. No emotional involvement
4. You don't have to drive your hand home
5. You don't have to fake an orgasm
6. You'll always have a date for New Year's
7. Easy cleanup

Masturbation: Hazards Of

1. Addiction
2. Nothing to talk about in the locker room
3. You might fall in love
4. Burn in Hell forever

Top 5 Turn-On Videos

1. **Monumental Knockers Volume II**
2. **Oralmania**
3. **High Price Spread**
4. **Sperm Busters**
5. **Talk to Me Dirty Part 2**

DE-VICES

Perfect Mates—Look for these at your local erotic boutique:

1. The Ultimate Caress

2. The Throbber

3. Pocket Pal

4. The Slave Girl Love Doll (inflatable)

5. Flexi-pump

REVENGE

Revenge is a dish best served cold.

SICILIAN PROVERB

▲ Revenge as a substitute for sex is rarely mentioned, simply because so few people are experienced enough with it to fully grasp its impact. All too often a novice will seek revenge instead of sex and wake up Saturday morning facing felony charges of attempted manslaughter—if he's lucky. Hundreds of men and women are behind bars simply because they knew more about getting laid than about getting even. Caution must be used. Patience and cunning must be employed. Also gloves.

For revenge to be successful (and therefore a worthy substitute for intercourse) three things are asked: a target, a course of action, and the faithful execution of that course of action. An error in any of these and you could find yourself being the love pet of the prison matron or being called "Sweetcakes" by an ax murderer named Maurice.

Look over your life, decide who (other than your parents) hurt you, lied to you, knifed you in the back, or blocked your advancement. Life's too short to dream about getting someone if you can't really do it, so begin by crossing off all those whom you can find no trace of. Not locating them is not a cause for disappointment—they could already be dead.

One at a time, devise revenges for those people still on your list. Brutal or fatal revenges certainly carry the highest satisfaction for you, but also the highest risk of capture, prosecution, and meeting Maurice. Choose wisely. A former boss, who fired you because of the impersonation you did of him at the Christmas party, does not deserve a car bomb. You may, however, with a clear conscience arrange for his wife to be photographed nude with a high school football team and send the photos to the company newsletter. Use your own best judgment.

TURN-ON CROSSWORD PUZZLE

(crossword grid)

For answers see p. 63.

▲ For those romantic evenings alone, this will help you warm up to yourself.

ACROSS:

1. Irregular past tense of "screw"
6. Mstbte. could be one
10. A great natural carpet to do it on
14. Heady scent
15. Lusty dance before wedding night
16. Use a paddle here
17. Even pine trees have secretions
18. Collections of sayings, such as "Give Me Liberty or Give Me Head"
19. Japanese tribe of hairy, half-naked savages
20. Postcoital position
23. Organ for aural sex
24. Played the voyeur
25. New York time

26. What Venus De Milo did for good sex
30. Sexy occupation, these days
32. Member of a trade whose product can increase sexual desire
33. How long you can keep it up
37. How you taste after hot sex
41. Having an affair with Madonna
44. Energy that heats you up all over
45. Do it Greek on this mountain
46. Once is not _____.
47. This Adderly has sax appeal
49. One does this to one's lover
51. Sexual sighs
54. Best place to pick up lover you can learn from
56. Premier who liked sashimi after sex
57. Hanging up phone so you can get back to what's in bed
63. Man with many women
64. Ibsen character who had something going on the side
65. Shunning masturbation
67. Mrs. Robinson, for instance
68. In a passion

69. Weather that permits more time in bed
70. What the Scotch have after sex
71. Exclamation as the point plunges home
72. Clean this and start with another partner

DOWN:

1. All-male association
2. Sometimes you eat it
3. Sub_____ (covertly, as with a tryst)
4. _____ the formalities (and get down to it)
5. Jennifer Beals was one
6. What you find in the shower after your lover has left
7. City of hearty sexual appetites
8. Boasts after the act
9. What Jack Nicholson often plays
10. What boxers do for foreplay
11. Get out of bed
12. Dating sheep or swine
13. What a magnificent body might do to you
21. Instrument of power in ancient days
22. Flooded in sexuality
26. Sets the bait
27. Item found in a sex guide

Answers

Across:

1. SCROD
6. ABBR
10. SAND
14. AROMA
15. HORA
16. PROA
17. ROSIN
18. ANAS
19. AINU
20. WATCHING CARSON
23. EAR
24. SAW
25. EST
26. DISARM
30. LAW
32. ALER
33. AEON
37. SALTY
41. PLAYING WITH FIRE
44. SOLAR
45. OSSA
46. ENOW
47. NAT
49. SCREWS
51. AHS
54. NEA
56. ITO
57. CUTTING THEM OFF

63. EMIR
64. NORA
65. ERROR
67. ROLE
68. IRED
69. RAINY

70. BREE
71. SASA
72. SLATE

DOWN:

1. SAR
2. CROW
3. ROSA
4. OMIT
5. DANCER
6. A HAIR
7. BONN
8. BRAGS
9. RASCAL
10. SPAR
11. ARISE
12. NO-NOS
13. DAUNT
21. HAMAN
22. AWASH

26. DAPS
27. ILLO
28. SEAL
29. ARYAN
31. WAFER
34. EGO
35. OWS
36. NIS
38. LINE
39. TROW
40. YEWS
42. IRANI
43. TASTE
48. TENNIS
50. COMERS
51. ACERB
52. HUMOR
53. STILE
55. AGORA

56. I HAD A
58. TREE
59. TRES
60. ORAL
61. FRIA
62. FONT
66. RYE

TURN-OFFS

Life holds many unexpected dangers, from being shot down behind enemy lines to an attractive partner begging for sexual intercourse. You must be prepared for all such terrifying events. Always carry an emergency survival kit: include a parachute, a small automatic weapon, cyanide tablets, and a list of proven sexual turn-offs in seven languages.

Memorize the following and then set it on fire or eat it. Just make sure these valuable turn-off secrets don't fall into the wrong hands.

PLACES WHERE YOU WON'T MEET ANYONE

▲ You're lonely. Depressed. Horny. You want to meet someone, spend some time together, make a new friend. Is that so much to ask? Yes! In your depressed condition, who knows what you'll do or try, and that includes sex. If you need to get out of your apartment, that's fine. Everyone deserves a little sunshine and fresh air. Just make sure you go someplace where there's no chance of meeting anyone you'd be remotely interested in. Stick to this list.

Shriners' convention

Dry-cleaners' convention

An emergency room

Your parents' condo or anyplace with your parents

A dating service

The Vatican

Any singles weekend

Buckingham Palace

Wrestlemania

Beirut, Lebanon

New York City subway

The Mayo Clinic

Any mah-jongg or canasta game

Any bingo game

Any bus in Los Angeles

The Mojave Desert in summer

The corner of Delancey and Clinton, New York City

The corner of Olympic and Flower, Los Angeles

For a more permanent place where you won't meet anyone, rent an apartment:

Under a bowling alley

Over a cheese store

Next to a landfill, bus depot or police station

Behind a tattoo parlor

MOST UNROMANTIC PLACES TO HAVE DINNER

▲ On your way to scoring, if dinner is first base, here's a group of places guaranteed to strike you out.

Any restaurant with:

A salad bar

A giant TV

Muzak

Pictures of food on a laminated menu

A special children's platter

Fluorescent lighting

A sign on the men's room that reads: CABALLEROS

An early-bird special

Drinks served in paper cups

Sandwiches named after famous people

Greyline tour connections

CITIES WITH NAMES TOO EMBARRASSING TO HAVE SEX IN

▲You *can* ask your country to do something for you. Just look around. This great land is crammed with cities whose names are so embarrassing you couldn't possibly have sex in them. Go to these places if you feel like having sex. As you and your date drive into the sleepy little hamlet of Blue Ball, Pennsylvania, you'll be stunned at how quickly your mind abandons thoughts of intercourse and begins wondering exactly what the town logo is.

Use the following cities as a starting point, but feel free to consult any Rand-McNally to map out your very own places to turn off.

Balls Ferry, California

Fort Deposit, Alabama

French Lick, Indiana

Twin Peaks, California

Beaver Dam, Kentucky

Licking, Missouri

Middlesex, New Jersey

Big Beaver, Pennsylvania

Intercourse, Pennsylvania

Keisters, Pennsylvania
Blue Ball, Pennsylvania
Hooker, Pennsylvania
Placentia, California
Cherry Valley, California
Golden Rod, Florida

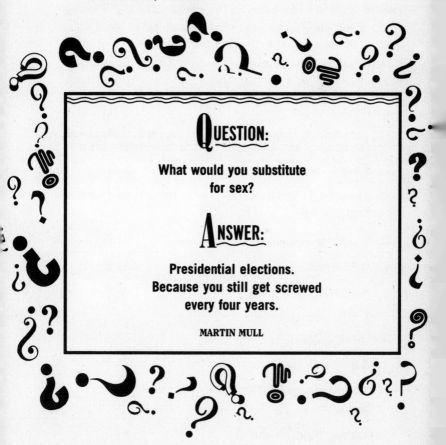

QUESTION:

What would you substitute
for sex?

ANSWER:

Presidential elections.
Because you still get screwed
every four years.

MARTIN MULL

WORST CITIES TO MEET SOMEONE IN

▲ Nothing puts a crimp in a budding relationship or kills it dead in its tracks like being in the wrong place at the wrong time. Poor choices to pursue relationships in (and thus exactly where you want to be) include war zones, refugee camps, cities with extremes in temperatures, cities where death is a big part of daily life, and any city on Barry Manilow's current tour.

TEN HOTTEST CITIES	AVERAGE TEMPERATURE
1. Tombouctou, Mali	84.7
2. Tirunelveli, Tamil Nadu, India	84.7
3. Khartoum, Sudan	84.6
4. Omdurman, Sudan	84.6
5. Madurai, Tamil Nadu, India	84.0
6. Niamey, Niger	84.0
7. Aden, S. Yemen	83.9
8. Tiruchchirappalli, Tamil Nadu, India	83.8
9. Madras, Tamil Nadu, India	83.5
10. Ouagadougou, Upper Volta	83.5

TEN COLDEST CITIES	AVERAGE TEMPERATURE
1. Ulan Bator, Mongolia	24.8
2. Chita, USSR	27.1
3. Bratsk, USSR	28.0
4. Ulan-Ude, USSR	28.9
5. Angarsk, USSR	29.7
6. Irkutsk, USSR	30.0
7. Komsomol'sk-na-Amure, USSR	30.7
8. Tomsk, USSR	30.9
9. Kemerovo, USSR	31.3
10. Novosibirsk, USSR	31.8

Fifteen U.S. Cities in Which You Are Most Likely To Die in a Motor Vehicle Accident (over 100,000 pop.)

1. San Bernardino, California
2. Lubbock, Texas
3. Nashville, Tennessee
4. Oklahoma City, Oklahoma
5. Fort Worth, Texas
6. Tucson, Arizona
7. Phoenix, Arizona
8. Beaumont, Texas
9. Corpus Christi, Texas
10. Kansas City, Missouri
11. Stockton, California
12. Kansas City, Kansas
13. Fresno, California
14. Dallas, Texas
15. Jacksonville, Florida

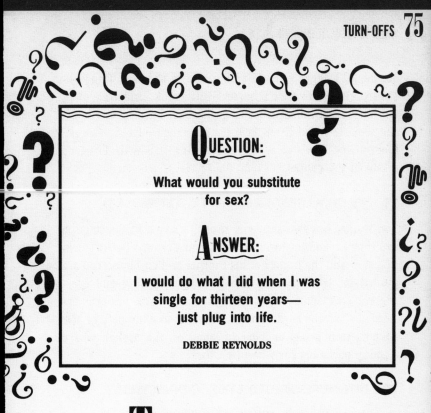

Qᴜᴇꜱᴛɪᴏɴ:

**What would you substitute
for sex?**

Aɴꜱᴡᴇʀ:

**I would do what I did when I was
single for thirteen years—
just plug into life.**

DEBBIE REYNOLDS

Tʜᴇ Mᴏꜱᴛ Uɴʀᴏᴍᴀɴᴛɪᴄ
Pʟᴀᴄᴇꜱ ɪɴ ᴛʜᴇ Wᴏʀʟᴅ

▲Vacations are notorious as breeding grounds for romance, lust, and sex. How can you protect yourself from beautiful views, sensuous breezes, hot nights, and tropical drinks? Select your vacation this year from among the following:

THE ROY ROGERS MUSEUM
(VICTORVILLE, CALIFORNIA)

An exciting monument, in the shape of an old cavalry fort, to Roy and his wife, Dale Evans. There's a twenty-four-foot statue of Trigger outside and inside is the real Trigger—stuffed, just like Dale's horse, Buttermilk, and their dog, Bullet. Also inside are wedding pictures, hunting and bowling trophies, and Roy's favorite powerboat. Keep a special lookout for Roy's clear acrylic bowling ball with Trigger's photo in the center.

TWITTY CITY (HENDERSONVILLE, TENNESSEE)

Twitty City has two souvenir shops, a snack bar, a stage, a multimedia auditorium/museum, and Conway Twitty's own mansion and the homes of his mother and children. You are guided on your tour by the endlessly giggling and ever-present specter of Twitty Bird, a country-and-western version of Tweetie Bird. You'll see eight-foot models of the singer's tour buses and get to stand on the asphalt where Conway parks his car when he's there.

THE NUT MUSEUM (OLD LYME, CONNECTICUT)

Run by the Nut Lady, Elizabeth Tashjian, the Nut Museum has every kind of nut, nutcrackers, nut sheet music, nut masks, and even Ms. Tashjian's own nut-theme sculptures. She claims, "Nuts are more than just snack treats, they're treats to the soul." She dreams of opening a thirty-two-acre Nut Theme Park on a waterfront, with a pier in the shape of a giant nutcracker holding a line of shops. Make sure you hear her a cappella version of "The Nut Anthem."

THE CYPRESS KNEE MUSEUM (PALMDALE, FLORIDA)

Built in 1951, this museum and its gift shop are designed to glorify the bizarrely twisted "knees" that grow up from the roots of cypress trees. The owner and founder, Tom Gaskins, has assembled a vast collection of knees from twenty-three states, each with its own sign that suggests a resemblance or celebrity for the knee. Make sure you find Flipper, Stalin, and "lady hippo wearing a Carmen Miranda hat." Tom himself boils and peels the knees and then licks off the wood fiber to give them that polished, satiny look.

TUPPERWARE MUSEUM (KISSIMMEE, FLORIDA)

The museum features the Tupperware Model Kitchen, where the refrigerator and cabinets are packed with only Tupperware. Every food has been removed from its store package and transferred into a Tupperware container. No bags, bottles, or cans exist in this world. Suggestions for new Tupperware items are welcomed.

HOOVER HISTORICAL CENTER (NORTH CANTON, OHIO)

This two-story museum is devoted to the inventiveness of the Hoover Vacuum Cleaner Company, which brought triple-action cleaning and the vacuum-cleaner headlight to mankind. Don't miss the antique machines and the original Hoover Model O.

ENTERPRISE SQUARE, USA (OKLAHOMA CITY, OKLAHOMA)

This is a $15-million glorification of the free-enterprise system and it's located on the campus of Oklahoma Christian College. A videotaped Bob Hope greets tour groups, who are led through such exhibits as the Great American Marketplace—where giant replicas of paper money have animated presidents' heads that talk and sing—and the Great Talking Face of Government, which shows tourists the problems that can arise when government oversteps its bounds, via a giant head with nine video screens. Be sure to see the World's Largest Functioning Cash Register.

BANANA MUSEUM (ALTADENA, CALIFORNIA)

The owner of the museum, Ken Bannister, believes bananas make people laugh and therefore feel good about themselves. He and the seven thousand members of the International Banana Club have collected thousands of banana-related items in the museum. They amuse one another by talking about how they earned Banana Merits or their Master of Bananistry degrees. Bannister hopes to make billions of people smile. Why not be one of them?

COLD SHOWERS

▲ Cave paintings show a stick figure with an erection jumping into a waterfall. Primal turn-off. Clean, inexpensive, and it's available to everyone. Timing, however, is important. You must know when to jump into the shower—too early in the date and all you'll be is clean, looking for someone to warm you up. Take a shower too late and the whole thing would be pointless—hot, cold, alone, together, vibrating massage, who cares? You've had intercourse and now you'll have to live with the consequences. To avoid this grim scenario in your life, study the following tips that will make you a more effective cold-shower taker.

WHEN TO TAKE A COLD SHOWER

After she's told you you're the most exciting man in the world

After he's given you an emerald bracelet

After he tells you he wants to meet your parents

After she answers the door in her bra and panties

After he says "I love you"

After she says "I want your body"

After you've taken a bath together

PLACES TO TAKE A COLD SHOWER

Your local YMCA/YWCA

Your parents' house

Someone else's apartment

The sprinkler in the front yard

Your high school locker room

Waterslide U.S.A.

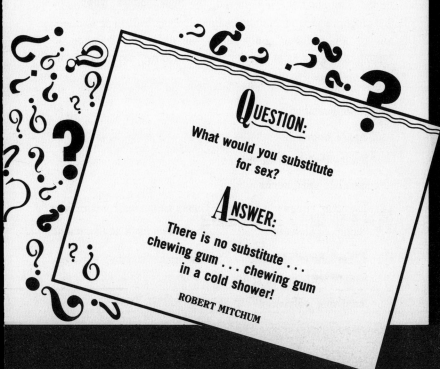

QUESTION:

What would you substitute for sex?

ANSWER:

There is no substitute . . . chewing gum . . . chewing gum in a cold shower!

ROBERT MITCHUM

CLOTHES

*You can add years to your
life by wearing your
pants backwards.*

JOHNNY CARSON, 1977

▲ Don't hesitate to use your appearance to turn off possible
sexual partners. Whoever said "clothes make the man"
left out the crucial final words, "an untouchable, sexless
nerd." The shoelace left untied, the torn fishnet stockings,
disturbing and unexplained stains, the misbuttoned shirt—
any or all of these could mean the difference between a
casual, deadly sexual encounter and a long, squeaky-clean
life of virtuous living.

Whenever possible, wear:

Space shoes

Pants that are too short

Sandals with socks

Elevator shoes   **Loose underwear with holes**

Saggy pantyhose   **Pants too high at the waist**

Pilling sweaters

Shirts with sweat spots

Anything polyester

Foods That Make You Unattractive

▲ You lead a busy life. There's no time to add another discipline or chore to your activity-filled day. So how can you, on a regular basis and with no extra effort, assure yourself of being unattractive to the opposite sex? The answer is simple: food. Not eating sloppily, although some spaghetti or spinach stuck to your cheek for hours will discourage even the most ardent fan. The secret is in what you eat itself—and the amount of gas that food can produce. Flatulence. It may well become the buzzword of the nineties. Extensive gas can produce abdominal pains, bloating, and distension—all terrific excuses for not having sex. Other foods can produce that classic reason for no coitus—a headache. Finally, the beauty that is bad breath cannot be ignored. What better way to turn someone off than to develop breath that makes people think something died in your mouth. By taking just a moment to deliberate on the foods you eat, you'll save hours and hours from the time you won't be having sex. Bon appetit!

Gas-Producing Foods

Onions	Peanuts	Cauliflower
Radishes	Eggs	Coffee
Baked beans	Malted milkshakes	Cola drinks
New apples	Soda waters	Beer
Cucumbers	Milk	Anything with bubbles
Lettuce	Melons	

I'VE GOT A HEADACHE!

Too much of these foods can often trigger a brain-splitter:

Red wine	Salami
Champagne	MSG
Chicken liver	Ham
Bacon	Hot dogs
Chocolate	Strong hard cheese

HOW TO DEVELOP REALLY BAD BREATH

Make sure you include one of these foods in every meal:

Garlic	Corn nuts
Onions	Coffee
Cheese	Milk
Peanut butter	Anchovies

TIME-SAVING TIPS

Never brush your teeth

Never floss your teeth

Never use a toothpick—leave food stuck between teeth

MONEY-SAVING TIP

Never go to the dentist

RECOMMENDED RECIPE

Breath of Death Sandwich
Spread peanut butter on one slice of white bread. Layer this with sliced Bermuda onion, dill pickle, and sardines. Top with another slice of bread. Serve immediately.

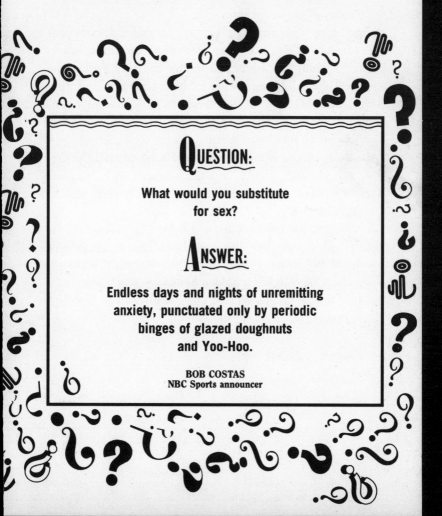

QUESTION:

**What would you substitute
for sex?**

ANSWER:

**Endless days and nights of unremitting
anxiety, punctuated only by periodic
binges of glazed doughnuts
and Yoo-Hoo.**

BOB COSTAS
NBC Sports announcer

SUNBURN

▲ Don't forget the old adage "Damage your skin, damage your relationship." You must never underestimate the effectiveness of a good, old-fashioned sunburn in turning off sexual appetites. Certainly your desire for bouncing, grinding, rubbing, sticky-hot sex will be eliminated by a thorough sunning that produces pain over 75 to 80 percent of your body. You'll want to nap in an Amana. As for your partner, how sexually attractive will he or she find a lobster-red, blistering, whimpering, cranky creature smeared with Noxema? You will never again hear the words *not tonight* said so quickly and firmly.

Not just any old sunburn you happen to pick up on the beach will do. Follow the guidelines below. They were developed by an expert panel of leathery-skinned sun worshippers. This plan has a hidden bonus—you're assured of a sex-free future for decades to come with all the repellent skin cancers you're bound to develop.

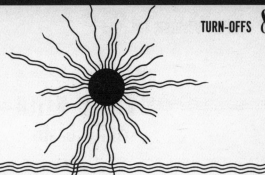

Sunburn Tips

Make sure your sun product does not contain benzophenone or oxybenzone. These ingredients block UVA.

Be certain that your lotion doesn't contain any paba, cinnamates, or octyl salicylate. These are UVB blockers that you want to avoid at all costs.

Insist on your product having no polymers as these allow the lotion to stay on longer when you're in the water or sweating.

The lotion of choice is your own mixture of baby oil and iodine. This, plus a sun reflector (for the rotisserie effect), is guaranteed to make your skin sizzle.

Demand a Sun Protection Factor of 0 to 2.

Choose the time and length you tan very carefully. A minimum of four hours in the direct sun every day is recommended. The best hours are from 10:00 A.M. to 2:00 P.M.

On your way home from the beach, finish off with a quick thirty minutes in a tanning salon. When you reach home, douse yourself with aftershave, cologne, or any alcohol-based liquid.

NIX 'N' MATCH— WORD GAME

▲A quiet Sunday afternoon at home. The two of you curled up cozily on the sofa, reading the paper or your favorite English authors. You get ideas. Sexual ideas. There's no reason on earth why you two won't be making bouncy-bouncy in a matter of seconds—unless you are prepared with a copy of the following word game (slipped into your novel or section of the paper) and you ask which word means "to cover or bury in dung." If your love object responds at all, he or she will return to reading faster than you can dot the *i* in *immerd*. No points for completing the game correctly—simply the pleasure and safety of being saved from having sex.

NIX 'N' MATCH

Match the words with their correct definitions. (Warning: The following word game is extremely gross but guaranteed to prevent sexual arousal.)

1. achor	8. gleet	15. smegma
2. acrotomophilia	9. immerd	16. fetor
3. caruncles	10. infibulation	17. mephitic
4. cock a grice	11. keck	18. pituitous
5. coprolagnia	12. merkin	19. puruloid
6. coprophagia	13. polysarcia	20. coprolith
7. crang	14. rhypophagy	21. rugose

a) excessive growth of the flesh; obesity

b) a strong offensive smell; fetidness

c) discharging or full of mucus

d) full of wrinkles, specifically plants having the veinlets sunken and the spaces between elevated

e) resembling pus

f) offensive to the smell; poisonous, noxious odors

g) a fatty or oily substance secreted by sebaceous glands of the prepuce and glans of the penis of most men

h) the eating of filth

i) a wig for the female genitals

j) to make a sound as if to vomit

k) a mass of hard fecal material

l) the prevention of intercourse before marriage by sewing or clasping together the labia majora, leaving a small opening for urination

m) to bury or cover with dung

n) an abnormal discharge of urethral mucus occurring in gonorrhea

o) the carcass of a whale after the blubber has been removed

p) the eating of feces, a symptom occasionally found in deteriorated schizophrenics

q) a medieval dish consisting of an old cock and a pig boiled together

s) the sexually arousing fantasy that one's lover is an amputee

t) a sexual disorder in which an individual repeatedly derives sexual excitement from handling feces, as well as from the sight, smell, and thought of feces

u) fleshy protuberances that hang around the bill of the male turkey

r) a scaly scalp eruption characteristic of the disease known as "scald-head"

THINGS TO WORRY ABOUT

▲Your analysis is complete. Your parents are dead. Your job is secure. You've met someone terrific; intimacy is a loving moment away. You're not even concerned about having sex. Why should you be? You've got nothing to worry about. Worrying would cause you to be impotent, unresponsive, or make you dress up like Mussolini the way you had to before your analysis was concluded. No, you really have nothing to worry about. Simply run down the following worries and then rest assured that you need never fret about sex again.

1. That small but constant pain in your stomach.

2. The birthday card you forgot to send to your brother.

3. How much money you have and how much you don't have.

4. How much hair will be on your pillow this morning.

5. Why don't your tires just blow out?

6. Exactly how many more days will you be alive?

7. What did your mother mean by "see you soon"?

8. If the cable guy came back during the day, how much stuff of yours could he steal before your neighbors called the police?

9. How much of your carotid artery does one slice of cheesecake block?

10. Is that tingling in your kidneys or your liver?

11. Can satanic cults afford your neighborhood?

12. Does anybody *really* love you?

13. What did your grandfather die of and is it genetic?

14. Who wants you dead?

15. Why do they chop everything up in Chinese food? What are they trying to hide?

16. Just how competent were the illiterate workers who built your building?

17. What keeps you from being blown off your balcony by a really strong wind?

18. How many people would come to your funeral?

19. How many of them would be happy?

20. How come there are only twenty things to worry about?

HOW TO TURN OFF THE WOMAN YOU WANT

1. Ask if you can share her Kleenex.

2. Talk about your past girl friends and show pictures.

3. Ask to borrow money.

4. Talk about your rashes.

5. Ask how much everything costs.

6. Discuss recent operations in detail and display scars.

7. Ask, "What's your sign?"

8. Ask to use the phone—then call Rome.

9. Ask her if she minds taking the bus to dinner.

10. Ask to see naked pictures of her.

11. Ask if there's Kaopectate in the house.

12. Brag about what a great lover you are.

HOW TO TURN OFF THE MAN YOU WANT

1. Be overly explicit in describing what you want sexually.

2. Be assertive and aggressive. Make the first move.

3. Call him five times a day.

4. Accept a date every time he asks. He will ultimately get bored and be less attentive—now that he's sure of you.

5. Tell him you love him. He will instantly withdraw.

6. Always be an hour late for dates.

7. Forget his name.

8. Talk a lot about your ex.

9. Ask, "When are we getting married?"

10. Talk about how underpaid he is at work.

11. Talk about how many orgasms you have during sex.

12. Talk about commitment.

13. Talk about:

his hairline	his junk
his penis size	your therapy
his belly	his therapy
his mother	his former wife or girl friend
his age	

S AFE PARTNERS

▲ It's time to review. Flip through once again and make sure you fully comprehend the chapters on asexuality, diversions, substitutes, and turn-offs.

If you no longer have any sexual cravings or feel that your desire has shriveled enough to be of no danger, read no further. You have mastered the art of sexual substitution. You are again ready to face the world of temptation. Hold your head high, walk confidently through any sexual situation, and sing something by Lerner and Lowe.

If, however, you feel unsure of yourself—still pitiful, weak, depraved, quivering and drooling at the mere thought of sex, unable to control those raging animal lusts any better than a stallion in a field, then this chapter is for you. If you are going to be sexually active, you must find a partner who's *safe*. A safe partner is that one special person with whom you are able to build such a rotten relationship that sex is the last thing on both of your minds. There are plenty of safe partners out there. Here are some tips on how to spot them.

A SAFE WOMAN

1. Sleeps with her dolls.
2. Vacuums on your first date.
3. Orders the most expensive item on the menu.
4. Sleeps with her pit bull.
5. Has bunk beds.
6. Refers to her underpants as "bloomers."
7. Is still doing EST.
8. Has a regular appointment at the hairdresser every Saturday.
9. Has hair between her eyebrows.
10. Goes to a beach topless—unnoticed.

A SAFE MAN

1. Is over thirty and still lives with his parents.
2. Calls you "Sugar."
3. Is always looking at himself in the mirror.
4. Has a pay phone in his car and a pay toilet at home.
5. Asks you to cut his meat.
6. Needs his "space."
7. Is a priest.
8. Wears Canoe, Old Spice, or Aqua Velva.
9. Owns a heating pad.

10. Has a tattoo that washes off.

11. Uses his sleeve instead of his handkerchief.

12. Blow-dries his hair before jogging.

13. Has a vanity license plate that reads: STUD 1.

14. Lives by the *Playboy* "Adviser."

Use the ancient art of astrology in your quest for the perfect partner with whom you will *not* want to have sex. If you follow the chart below, you'll find the one person who's wrong for you—they will disappoint you or you'll infuriate them. You'll be mutually incompatible, so there's not even the slightest chance of a relationship developing, let alone a brief affair or a one-night stand. You'll find the question "What's your sign?" can now be an important tool in *not* getting it.

ASTROLOGICAL SIGN	WORST PARTNER
Aries	Cancer or Capricorn
Taurus	Leo or Aquarius
Gemini	Virgo or Pisces
Cancer	Libra or Aries
Leo	Taurus or Scorpio
Virgo	Gemini or Sagittarius
Libra	Cancer or Capricorn
Scorpio	Leo or Aquarius
Sagittarius	Virgo or Pisces
Capricorn	Aries or Libra
Aquarius	Taurus or Scorpio
Pisces	Gemini or Sagittarius

TURN-OFF CROSSWORD PUZZLE

For answers see p. 97.

▲This crossword puzzle should keep you sex-free for months.

ACROSS:

1. Fish that stinks after three days

6. AIDS, for example

10. Gets in K-Y at beach

14. Yummy armpit odor

15. If you can't bear to dance cheek to cheek

16. In Indonesia, you can watch Gavin MacLeod on *The Love*_____.

17. Something to rub on your sinstrument

18. Collection of sayings, such as "When the prick stands up, the brain goes to sleep."

19. Member of a tribe that practices lip-tattooing

20. What many of you are doing before, during, and after sex

23. Stick it in here
24. "Better safe than sorry" is one
25. Weekend bladder-control therapy
26. To remove yourself from an unwanted embrace
30. In many states, fellatio can bring this down on your head
32. Beverage maker; former whaler until a killer bit off part of his whang
33. How long a bad lay stays with you
37. Why hypertensive girl friend won't swallow sperm
41. Screwing Richard Pryor
44. Eclipse when the moon butts in
45. Greek mountain where shepherds first found sheep attractive
46. Old way of saying that's enough, which is still what you should be saying
47. _____ King Cole (performer who played with himself)
49. How one messes up a platonic relationship
51. Try massage, not sex, for these
54. Organization of pedagogues, not pederasts
56. Former prime minister of a country where all scenes of frontal nudity are banned

57. Drastic method to ensure celibacy in men
63. Eunuch employer
64. Author of *Heartburn* and a few wrecked relationships
65. Going to bed without a condom
67. The Hunchback of Notre Dame, for one
68. The opposite of slow and seductive
69. Type of afternoon for staying in a moviehouse
70. In the soup, in Scotland
71. Fencer's cry just before he castrates you
72. This with fingernails stops everything

DOWN:

1. Organization where chances of meeting women are nil
2. Humiliating hors d'oeuvre
3. Sub——— (done secretly, as with disgusting sexual acts)
4. Leave out that heavy date for tonight
5. Michael Jackson is such a good one of these, he can almost fake having a gender
6. Disgusting item to find on your soap
7. European capital
8. How a schmuck completes intercourse

9. Buckwheat, sleeping around
10. Do this to relieve frustration
11. With a full bladder, your penis does this to greet the morning sun
12. Sexual escapades, today
13. What the threat of AIDS should do to you
21. He had long ears, not a long organ
22. In a used rubber, sperm is _____
26. Fishes with the guys (good sex-substitute)
27. See page _____ in this book
28. Everybody got fucked in the seventh reel
29. Hitler frowned on masturbation; he preferred this kind of master nation
31. Eat this instead of a schlong
34. Don Juan's is too big
35. Sounds from a cactus love nest
36. Effeminate little pixy
38. Don't fall for any
39. To believe, like in the old days when sex was fun
40. Trees for mees and _____
42. This citizen blames America for his straying wife
43. Larry Flynt has none

48. Ball smashing
50. Those who can't hold it in
51. The way an ejaculation tastes
52. Necessary substitute for sex
53. Subway nutcracker
55. Where Greeks bought gifts
56. "_____ headache" (good excuse for last night)
58. Bohemian club urinal
59. Two girls and a guy in Madrid
60. A test of sex
61. A ballbusting Norse goddess
62. Dive into this for a cold shower
66. You can catch something here

Answers

Across:

1. SCROD
6. ABBR
10. SAND
14. AROMA
15. HORA
16. PROA
17. ROSIN
18. ANAS
19. AINU
20. WATCHING CARSON
23. EAR
24. SAW
25. EST
26. DISARM
30. LAW
32. ALER
33. AEON
37. SALTY
41. PLAYING WITH FIRE
44. SOLAR
45. OSSA
46. ENOW
47. NAT
49. SCREWS
51. AHS
54. NEA
56. ITO
57. CUTTING THEM OFF

63. EMIR
64. NORA
65. ERROR
67. ROLE
68. IRED
69. RAINY

70. BREE
71. SASA
72. SLATE

DOWN:

1. SAR
2. CROW
3. ROSA
4. OMIT
5. DANCER
6. A HAIR
7. BONN
8. BRAGS
9. RASCAL
10. SPAR
11. ARISE
12. NO-NOS
13. DAUNT
21. HAMAN
22. AWASH

26. DAPS
27. ILLO
28. SEAL
29. ARYAN
31. WAFER
34. EGO
35. OWS
36. NIS
38. LINE
39. TROW
40. YEWS
42. IRANI
43. TASTE
48. TENNIS
50. COMERS
51. ACERB
52. HUMOR
53. STILE
55. AGORA

56. I HAD A
58. TREE
59. TRES
60. ORAL
61. FRIA
62. FONT
66. RYE

BELIEVE IT OR NOT

Never having sexual intercourse again is unnatural— unless you're a single-celled animal. Life is filled with many such bizarre and seemingly cruel occurrences. How else would you explain the success of Sergio Valente? This is an era of overturned beliefs and historic changes for mankind. You must decide for yourself about the necessity of sex. There are two paths: *believe it or not.*

- **S**eventy-five percent of women who had affairs with their bosses wouldn't do it again. Neither would their bosses.

- **F**orty-seven percent of American men enjoy sex more than money.

- **T**wenty-six percent of American women say they enjoy sex more than money.

- **T**wenty-five percent of American married couples say they argue about sex or adultery.

- **G**irls can avoid pregnancy by jumping up and down after sex.

- **F**our hundred million condoms are now sold annually in the United States.

- **L**obsters are celibate.

- **G**reen M&Ms make you horny.

- **B**righam Young was asexual.

- **A**bsinthe is an antiaphrodisiac and is responsible for France's population decline.

- **T**he word *penis* did not exist in Shakespeare's time. It first appeared in the English language seventy-seven years after the Bard died.

- **T**here is no woman on this earth who doesn't believe her breasts are too small, big, flat, round, pointed, or saggy.

- **A** recent survey revealed that 90 percent of married men masturbate and the other 10 percent are lying.

- **A**nal intercourse is illegal in England and parts of the United States.

Average Number of Sperm per Ejaculation:
Golden Hamster—3,450
Rat—82,500,000
Human—500,000,000
Sheep—3,000,000,000
Swine—45,000,000,000

- **T**he word *vagina*, first used in the English language in 1682, comes from the same Latin root as *vanilla*.

- **D**uring the Victorian age, polite society called a chicken breast a bosom, banned advertisements that would reveal that ladies' underwear had legs, and put crinolines on piano legs.

- In 1926, Wilhelm Reich published *Function of the Orgasm*, in which he said that failure to achieve orgasm caused mental and physical diseases. He later claimed that masturbation could combat cancer.

- Celibacy increases life expectancy by ten years.

- Tigers' sex organs pickled in brandy and crushed tiger bones are the ingredients in a Chinese aphrodisiac, Tiger Wine.

- The makers of Trojan now offer a wallet-sized gold plastic card that reads: MAY I PLEASE HAVE A BOX OF TROJAN BRAND CONDOMS? for those too shy to ask out loud in their neighborhood drugstore.

INFIDELITY AND INCOME

INCOME	% OF MEN UNFAITHFUL	% of WOMEN UNFAITHFUL
Under $5,000	16	29
$5,000–$10,000	23	35
$10,000–$20,000	31	44
$20,000–$30,000	47	45
$30,000–$40,000	54	49
$40,000–$50,000	64	44
$50,000–$60,000	68	47
$60,000 +	70	41

NUMBER OF SEXUAL PARTNERS FOR MEN

None	3%
1–5	30%
5–10	17%
10–25	24%
25–50	13%
50+	12%

YOUR SEX LIFE AND AGING

AGE	ANGLE OF ERECTION
20	10% above horizontal
30	20% above horizontal
40	Slightly above horizontal
50	Slightly below horizontal
70	25% below horizontal

YOUR FREQUENCY OF ORGASM

AGE	ORGASMS PER YEAR
20	104 (49 solo)
30	121 (10 solo)
40	84 (8 solo)
50	52 (2 solo)
60	35 (4 solo)
70	22 (8 solo)

- Two antidepressants, clomipramine and trazodone, have unusual side effects—they cause yawning spells that produce "irresistible sexual urges" and even orgasms. Just from yawning.

- Philosopher Immanuel Kant couldn't. He died a virgin in 1804.

- Attila the Hun died in action—in bed.

- Félix Faure, French president (1884–1889) died in a specially designed sex chair with his mistress.

- Pope Leo VIII died of a stroke while committing adultery.

- Seven hundred Americans have been conceived in test tubes.

- Hugh Hefner lost his virginity at age twenty-three.

- Ten percent of all men have faked at least one orgasm.

- Ninety-three thousand five hundred women have had their breasts surgically enlarged.

- Forty-nine thousand six hundred women have had their breasts surgically reduced.

- Americans spend $40 million a day on prostitutes.

- Elephants masturbate with their trunks.

- Four hundred fifty thousand Americans were conceived by artificial insemination.

- Eighteen percent of men have sexual trouble every year.

- You can still buy chastity belts. David Renwick of Sheffield, England, hand-forges custom-made iron chastity belts to your specification for about eighty dollars apiece. Most clients order the belts for decoration or fun, though your order includes two keys with each belt.

FINAL ACT

Our goal has been to bring you to a state of mind-numbing exhaustion that can be found only in a life lived without the hazards of sex. If you have not attained this level of nonsexuality, then your last—and only—hope is to take this book and squeeze it firmly between your legs.

ABOUT THE AUTHOR

Barry Sand is a television producer and writer. His credits include the innovative, Emmy-award-winning *SCTV Comedy Network* and *Late Night with David Letterman*. Mr. Sand, a graduate of the University of Pennsylvania's Wharton School, lives in both New York City and Los Angeles, California.